For Frank

Read & thanks for your input -

Ray

FREEMASONRY...

WHENCE DID IT
TAKE ITS RISE?

Raymond Hudson

British Library Cataloguing in Publication Data

A catalogue record for this book is available
from the British Library

ISBN-13: 978-1-913751-09-8

Cover Illustration:
Knights Templar Battle Flag:
Beau Seant

CONTENTS

CHAPTER ONE
INTRODUCTION

Having been an active member of Freemasonry for the past 35 years, in which I have been able to pursue activities that my professional occupations and family obligations placed the justifiable restrictions on, I have managed to reach a senior position in all the mainstream Masonic Orders that proliferate within this magnanimous Organisation, plus many more beyond this so called mainstream.

I have pursued my passion for history and research, to understand the why and wherefore of everything I have done and currently do within masonry. Whenever I receive an answer that does not make sense to me I always try and find an answer that lies comfortable for me rather than accept what at first may appear a fobbing off, because the interlocutor has no real answer, or supplies one that holds little sense. Or the reply, as it often is, "Oh it is in the book", or "You will discover later as you progress" or "That is how we have always done it", these proved to be merely obfuscations for a total lack of knowledge.

Naturally I became a pain with my constant questions and queries to anyone that would listen. Even as a youngster I needed to know what Barn Owls were called before there were barns, as I knew that the animal existed long before barns were created. It was many years before I actually found the true answer, and it came from a 12 year old lad while I was attending a Birds of Prey exhibition. This proved to me that answers can be found in the most unexpected places, and, most importantly, they are there waiting to be found if you have patience and diligence.

In a short period of approximately 5 years as a member

of the Craft, I embarked on many years of research and was eventually called to present whatever knowledge I had gained regarding its ceremonies and ritual in a lecture that, (I was told,) proved most useful and necessary to all who listened. So useful that it resulted in the publication of my first Masonic book entitled "So you think you know about Freemasonry". It proved so successful that I felt impelled to approach the Holy Royal Arch in the same manner. This book "So you think you know about the Chapter" enjoyed a similar success. Both these books plainly demonstrated to me that my direct but detailed approach in explaining the meaning, understanding and history of Freemasonry was not only needed but greatly appreciated. There were and still are countless worthy books explaining the countless Masonic themes, history and meanings but somehow and for reasons not really known by me, appreciation for my approach seems to be greatly received.....long may it continue.

During my Masonic career I have tried earnestly to discover the origin of this wonderful Society and Fraternity. It is so highly regarded by those who are fortunate enough to be it's members, so widely spread over the four quarters of the globe, it contains so many fascinating and diverse ceremonies that I find it difficult to believe that it suddenly appeared around the 1600-1700's. Most of the ceremonies conducted within the Freemasonic network are based upon stories from the Bible, and mainly from the Old Testament. Those Orders governed by the United Grand Lodge of England namely The Craft and The Holy Royal Arch both have their origin in the Old Testament.

The Orders that proliferate the rest of mainstream Freemasonry are to a large degree governed by The Mark Grand Lodge of England situated at St. James's. The balance are individually governed by their respective authorities.

The majority of these Orders each reflect and detail an incident or moral principle from either the Old or either the New Testaments. Sadly there are only two original and strictly English Orders within the whole pantheon of mainstream Freemasonry, which poses the obvious question; Why should Freemasonry have been created in England 300-400 years ago and yet contain only 2 purely English Orders that were only created within the last 25 years. Surely our English culture and history contains just as many moral principles and tenets of equal value to that contained in the Holy Books.

Within Masonic teachings it is widely held, although not definitively, that our entire world wide system emanated from either the Medieval builders or the Guilds or even some other situation depending on the researches of the particular author.

Therefore the arguments that proliferate concerning this question are many and varied, and have been discussed in numerous volumes by countless notable scholars. Each bringing something fresh and of value in their work, but somehow failing to connect all the links in one study. I hope, in my small way, to redress this situation, or at least to provide a few more links to your existing chain.

Of all the discussions and opinions regarding the origins of Freemasonry, there are three that enjoy dominance over the rest.

1). That it rose from the operative skills, and over the centuries gradually became speculative, due to the diminishing need for operative skills, as technology and construction evolved.

2). That it emanated from the Guilds and Liveries within the City of London.

3). That it was brought from the East to the West through the auspices of the Knights Templar.

Looking intently at the first argument, there are many,

many good reasons for taking this view. Naturally our ritual leans heavily on the artisan skills of building stately and superb edifices, and equates them to the building of a man. We call ourselves MASONS. We speculate on many aspects of this skill, and make many allusions to this special craft. Many respected researchers fall into this trap, which, by its very content, is easy to do. But I hope to prove that Freemasonry did not evolve directly from this admirable craft, but was itself grafted on to it to disguise its originality, for very poignant reasons.

Think of yourself, for the moment, as a medieval apprentice mason, serving a seven year apprentice under a proven skilled Master Mason. During this period, you eat, sleep and dream every aspect of this skilled operative craft. Learning and practising every skill and art involved in Masonry. Demonstrating in stages the different skills you have learned. At the end of this very arduous and intense training period, you are expected to present to your master a piece of commissioned work involving all the different skills acquired over this seven year period. This was called your "Masters-Piece" or masterpiece. If your piece of skill passed the very strict standards of craftsmanship expected, you were accepted as a Master Craftsman, and could go out into the world and make your mark. You would either set yourself up on your own, or more likely travel to one of the many large building projects going on at that time, and there were many, Churches, Cathedrals and Castles being built all over the country. Having arrived at one of these intended structures, and received employment, your ability and skill would be discovered by the quality of your work, and no other way. If you lied at the interview by professing to be better than you actually were, this would be immediately shown up by your lack of actual skill in the finished product. For as an apprentice you would not be shown or instructed in a higher skill until you had fully mastered the previous one. As these structures took anything from five to a hundred years to complete, any cowan or impostor would soon be discovered.

The point I am trying to make is that there is no need for any passwords or penalties, as there was nothing to protect in the operative skills, you had either mastered them or you had not, and the standard of your work would have been the governing factor and not your knowledge of certain passwords. There may well have been a sort of hierarchy or fraternal comradeship among the operative masons themselves that may have required a password, but surely would not have merited a severe penalty of death in some form. It was the standard of your work that decided your employment and scale of wages. As a modern example, in the Craft, if a fellowcraft had knowledge of the Master Masons word, and tried to pass himself as a Master Mason, it would not be too long before the genuine Master Masons became suspicious of his lack of knowledge of the ritual and rubric of the Third Degree. Once discovered he would be quickly dismissed. The same must have applied to the ancient operatives. In those days of much-demanded operative masonry skills the work was usually governed by an ecclesiastic person, as being the only one who could read or write, and as the building was usually a Church or some other Holy place, for the employment of the right person for the right job required the Ecclesiastic would have to know the various masonic words for the Apprentice, Fellow of the Craft and Master Mason. This completely belies the secrecy required within Masonic ceremonial.

So, as romantic as the thought may seem, and as romantic as some masonic writers and observers try to make it, it does not seem logical to me for the need for passwords or the importantly stressed penalties. I was, and still am, convinced that there was a very much more serious importance applied to these aspects of the modern Craft. Therefore, for these reasons, I dismiss the possibility of these origins.

Giving similar intense study to the second argument, I find there are too many historic and chronological differences for this point of view to have lasting merit. Although the Guild system is of ancient lineage, and is of a very similar physical structure, and holds many Masonic moral aspirations with similar respect, I cannot accept that Freemasonry rose from these fine institutions.

The Guilds were formed as a sort of protection for the members and as some sort of recourse for the customer. They were able to control quality and price, much the same as some Trade Federations do today. The Guilds also supervised the apprenticeships, which included a moral aspect towards oneself and the community. Also the guilds laid a very heavy stress on religious aspects, especially Christianity, something the Craft has studiously avoided since its supposed inception, and there is a very sound reason for this avoidance. Like the operatives there was no serious reason for the guilds to instigate passwords or even penalties, like those relating to the Craft. Having been awarded the Freedom of the City of London myself, in 1974, it is my belief that the Guilds borrowed some-what from the structure of Freemasonry. I do not intend, in this book, to expand further on this aspect, as my main aim is to put the point of Freemasonry and its rise, and not the City Guilds. So for the similar reasons stated, I have to dismiss this possibility with the same enthusiasm as I did the first.

So finally we arrive at the third possibility, which obviously must be the origin that I favour. That Freemasonry took its rise from the Knights Templar has, after many years of study and research, become positive for me for many many historic reasons, which I shall now proceed relate to you.

In detailing the development of Freemasonry - which I firmly believe did not suddenly appear but instead evolved, (and that very slowly) due to circumstance and events - we see the organisation morphing, by slow degrees, into the incredible Fraternity that we have today.

In order to ensure that my final logical conclusion has brevity and provenance I must invite the reader to journey with me right back to the beginning of human time and advance through the ages and cultures that have been an integral part in the developing system that we practise today as Freemasonry.

Within Masonic ritual and ceremony stories contained in the Old Testament are utilised to emphasise particular moral attributes that are as important and worthwhile today as they were when first related in the said Old Testament. Noah and the Great Flood, Abraham, Moses, Jacob, the Twelve Tribes of Israel, the most important building known as King Solomon's Temple etc, etc. In fact, within modern day Masonic lectures a claim is made that "…..Freemasonry has ever borne an affinity to Ancient Egypt…..", so it makes total sense to investigate these ancient times for clues as to their credibilty and use within a modern organisation.

Every aspect of these ancient times must be examined and considered in their relevence to our pursuit, and in doing this I will endeavour to make the journey as light as is sensibly possible, not losing any of its important value and at all times relating its value within our Masonic structure and content, proving by logical conclusion that Freemasonry evolved from time immemorial and openly revealed itself around the 16th century.

Please enjoy the read.

RAY HUDSON September 2020

CHAPTER 2
BELIEF SYSTEMS

We have to begin our quest at the time Homo Sapiens became fully developed to their present physical state. Our tails have gone, brains are fully developed and our speech is much more than grunts and groans and is becoming more tonally expressive. We are beginning to think about ourselves and more importantly about our environment. We are socialising in groups and beginning the early stages of being civilised. There are no buildings of any description, therefore shelter is found wherever and whenever it is needed. The biggest development at this time is Fire, its production, use and control. Fire must have been observed in its natural state of spontaneous combustion, wherefrom its warmth was felt, and any animals that became trapped within a fire it was noticed and its difference in taste must have been appreciated. From this, over time, was learned the use and control of fire. Subsequently time and experiment incorporated the use of Air and Water, the former in keeping the fire going and the latter in extinguishing it. Earth was appreciated as an abundant commodity which together with water made mud which dried by the warmth of fire and became hard. Here we have in the most simplest terms the developing use of the four elements of life. Namely Fire, Air, Earth and Water such as are currently revered within modern Freemasonry.

Fire had the greatest of uses for the peoples of those times in that it cooked meat allowing for it to be preserved in some way so that further travel in hunting could be achieved. Fire could also be used to keep wild animals away from the settlement, as well as creating a central point at which many could sit around and socialise creating long opportunities for talking to each other and discussing the many things that greatly affected their lives. From this, speech began to progress to a particularly sophisticated level relative to those times.

Now we have a situation where some began to notice that the Sun was necessary to preserve and nurture life and vegetation. The consistency of the appearance of the Sun, not only appearing to rise from the same place every morning, but also its disappearance in another place in the evening. Talks around the fire must have occurred and questions where asked as to its consistency. Also discussions were held regarding the other wonders of nature which we, in our day, take entirely for granted. Furthermore there must have been talks about "who are we" and "how were we created" together with "why are we here". These sort of talks must have gone on for millennia.

As groups developed and situations greatly improved, crude structures that imitated the natural formations of nature began to be constructed and life began to develop at a fantastic and rapid creative pace. With this improvement in everything the talks around the fire began to become more intricate. The business of staying alive was made easier so minds wandered into other areas,

Amongst these groups, as is always the case, even today, there were a few natural opportunists who believed that if convincing answers could be supplied, supported by examples proved in nature, then in the absence of any other explanation, what was proffered would be accepted and believed, and the suppliers of these explanations would be revered for their apparent greater knowledge. This was not the beginnings of religion, that was to come much later but it was, although quite crude in its beginnings, a belief system of sorts. Throughout every group these deliverers of explanations become known as Magi, Shaman, Elders, Teachers, and were respected, regarded and treated accordingly with gifts and offerings which meant that they had to do less of the menial tasks that survival demanded in those times.

There were also those that studied the regularity of events in nature, the seasons, the plants, the sky, especially the night sky noting that the same stars appeared in the same place every night, and that they moved across the sky in a rhythm that almost transcended explanation. After a period of time these circumstances in nature and the heavens began to be conjoined by these Magi and Elders and woven together to strengthen the power of the understandings that were being put to the populace who were bereft of any knowledge other than that required for natural survival.

Eventually, in a similar manner as the Magi and Elders, some individuals began creating shelters using the natural materials laying abundant in their surroundings, forming shapes and designs that they observed in nature itself. Gradually stone was found and used together with wood and leaves and any other natural material that proved to assist in strengthening the structures erected. These developments were produced by observing natural events in plants and trees , and of course the habits of some animals that created crude shelters to protect their young.

Natural instincts like the greater physical strength and body size in the males, and with the very strong maternal instinct in the females, made leadership a natural choice. The strong hunter gatherer capabilities of the male coupled with the natural maternal tendencies of the female made the adoption of their specific roles naturally obvious and accepted without question. (Although history proves that, over time, there were and are unique exceptions in both the male and female to the above paragraph).

So with some regular organisation, crude structures for accommodation, cooking and the ability to preserve some foodstuffs, and a few other resultant situations that were naturally created by the development of the above, what we might call leisure time comparatively became more readily available. From this came further developments in language, which naturally produced more questions and a quest for more explanations, making a more difficult task for the Magi and Elders to maintain their status. It was the same then as it is now. If you give people knowledge, whether true or false, that knowledge will be used as a stimulus to explore further. So something much more detailed and acceptable had to be supplied, and it was. The Magi's, Elders and Teachers etc, came up with physical representations for every tangible, intangible, active and passive aspect of life in all its myriad of forms. These were known then, as they remain to this day as, GODS!!

CHAPTER 3
G O D S   A N D   R E L I G I O N

The Magi and their various equivalents around the well dispersed settlement areas of the then known world went further and stressed not only the Gods but also their interaction between themselves and with the human populace. The various penalties and afflictions that would be delivered should they wander from the particular instructions and principles required by their respective God were strictly applied, enforced and accepted and adhered to. These instructions were not delivered by the Gods themselves but by their intermediaries, the Magi, Elders etc.

A different God was created for every aspect of the life as it was known at that time, and duality was subtly being introduced, so that evil gods and divine Gods accommodated both sides of the spectrum. Generally most Gods took the form of a human as this form was easily related to by the congregation who were still fairly ignorant of knowledge. So we can legitimately say that Man created God in his own image. Over time as the knowledge in the congregation increased, the questions became more intricate, and the answers supplied equalled the intricacies of those questions. Again, for a long time, the congregation became satisfied and adherent.

We have now arrived loosely at that time when the various belief systems changed to become what we now call RELIGION.

They did not change simultaneously throughout the world, or overnight, but over a long period of time, a slow and gradual process, some taking much longer than others to reach this point. There are in most religions many similarities especially in the creation stories, which proves that some aspects of one religion, or even many religions, were grafted onto others to create more impact. This happened more often as travel became more increasingly prevalent throughout the world.

Gilgamesh and Enkidu slay the Bull of Heaven

If a simple study is made of the many early religions and their sagas or epics like "The Epic of Gilgamesh", duplication and insertion of stories and motifs can be better appreciated.

Even in the Mayan Indian religion their God Quetzalcoatl came out of the water, and the flood story to some degree is also quoted, and that is the other side of the world compared to the Holy Land.

As a simple example let us start with the Sumerians and their Belief System, within time, and making use of travel,

Quetzalcoatl Emerging

some of their system was borrowed. shall we say, by the Assyrians and grafted on to their belief system, which was then, by means of similar reasons of time and travel, partly grafted on to the belief system of the Phoenicians, and if this theory is continued through the Arab nations to the Hebrew nation the progressions and similarities of the independent belief systems throughout that part of the world can be appreciated and understood.

--ooOoo---

It cannot be denied that the Hebrew nation is at the root of the three most prolific and adhered to religions of the world, namely Judaism, Christianity and Islam. (

They are all Abrahamic faiths and are widely and academically known as Peoples of the Book, as all three religions follow the stories contained in the Bible.

The original and widely appreciated creator of the Jewish faith and therefore, although indirectly, both its offspring faiths of Christianity and Islam, must be ...MOSES. The acknowledged author of the first five books of the Old Testament.

This individual is most highly regarded within Freemasonic ritual and ceremonies, and in some circumstances "toasted" as one of our Great and Illustrious Founders. The floor on which all the ceremonial work isconducted is known as "The MOSAIC Pavement". The word MOSAIC simply means "In the style of Moses" as Archaic means in the style of the Ancients and Judaic means in the style of the Jews. The term originates from the biblical story that Moses was asked to build the first Tabernacle in the desert. It was made from Goat skin and goat hair, no actual stone masonry was used because it had to be portable. So Moses went into the desert and gathered up a load of stones and laid them on the floor of the Tabernacle in a regular pattern to create a more reverential and solemn respect. Ever since that event any stones laid in a pattern are called MOSAIC or in the style of MOSES.

This now brings us to a much closer look at the particular area that has had the most religious influence throughout the world, and I mean The Holy Land or The Fertile Crescent . In this connection I believe the best place to start is with EGYPT, who were at the time of discussion at its strongest in power and influence and the original birthplace and home of this acknowledged Masonic "Great and Illustrious Founder" of Freemasonry.....MOSES.

But before progressing to the inimitable character of Moses, we should examine the power and force of Religion itself, which was firmly established, in many forms throughout the world at the time of Moses. Through this appraisal, understanding can be better achieved as to religion's power and force, and the manner in which that power was utilised to encourage compliance. In true reality the word RELIGION is sadly mis-applied. Religion is not the object of the individual's relationship with whatever God or Gods that he reveres to or with. That is FAITH, and therefore all the so called known religions such as Judaism,

Christianity, Islam and Buddhism etc., are actually Faiths. RELIGION is actually the conduit through which we learn and understand our particular chosen FAITH. Although I am against the continuous use of bad grammar, I will continue to use the word RELIGION in the manner in which its general acceptance is used, hopefully to minimise confusion.

Religion has been found to be possibly the most powerful tool to command loyalty and sacrifice. The power of its reward or punishment systems truly command the greatest devotion and dedication. History records and demonstrates some of the greatest acts of faithful dedication and on the other side the most atrocious acts of brutality that can ever be imagined within the most fervent mind. The greatest sacrifice in Christianity must be acknowledged to be the Crucifixion of Jesus Christ, also the dedication and devotion of individuals such as Joan of Arc, Lawrence the Martyr, all the canonised Saints, Mother Therese et al. There are many similar examples in all the other faiths such as Mahatma Ghandi, Dalai Lama, this book could be filled with such individuals from all the religions that proliferate our world, but just a few examples will suffice to make the point. Conversely history records and demonstrates much of the inhumanities to man that have been inflicted in the name of religion. Consider the Conquistadores and their brutal treatment of the Aztecs, Incas and the Mayan Indians inflicting their religion on them and then plundering their gold and other material things. Also the Christian Missionaries to the African countries who went to convert the "savages" from their pagan and heathen beliefs with an attitude akin to "you will stop worshiping your God of the rain who nurtures your fields and enables you to provide food, or your God of the Sun who ripens your fruits and herbal plants, and you will worship a new God that walks on water and turns water into wine, if not, we will kill you". It sounds a bit blunt and crude but it certainly contains the power of the message I am trying to convey. We must not forget the acts of Adolf Hitler and the persecution of the Jews. Even in this our modern times the power within some Muslims in their understanding of the messages within Islam can drive them to acts that, in completing them results in their own death. The power of Faith is a powerful tool that can be used for good or, on occasion, bad. At some time or another throughout history both potentials have been exploited and experienced by all the known faiths/religions.

Countries, Empires or Regimes have been seen to use this powerful tool to achieve whatever their particular aim was, for instance, it is acknowledged that:

Constantine the Great in his unification of the Roman Empire realised that many of his Christian soldiers would rather die for their faith than they would for their Emperor, so he claimed to be one of them and obtained undying support from those soldiers, bringing for him the success he desired and aimed for. Also to prevent him sending out his armies, which was a huge cost factor, to quell the religious riots, he called the religious leaders together at Nicea in 325AD and forced them to come to an agreement which resulted in Christianity becoming the religion of the Roman Empire and eventually spread throughout the known world. This is just one example as there were many great leaders who realised the power of faith and strategically used it in their favour. Religion has proved to be used as simply another tool of war. Despite what I have written here and what exists as proof in world history we should not use our very modern moral judgement on events that occurred in the historical past or even pre-historic past, attitudes and morals were so much different in those days. We can only hope that the lessons that history set out to teach us do not go unheeded.

I hope I have given a clear explanation, albeit in the simplest of terms, of the power of faith/religion and how its use has been exploited throughout history by great leaders, and of course by the religious leaders of the respective faiths. It is now time to return to Egypt at the time of Moses and fully explore both factors as they have and will continue to have a great influence on this literary quest.

CHAPTER 4
BACK TO EGYPT

Egypt was for long periods in time a most powerful and influential nation. Its understanding of the stars, its knowledge of construction exemplified in the most complicated structure of the pyramids, which we now know where not only built for the entombment of Pharaohs and their families, but also as planetary observatories, so that the essential flooding of the Nile could be observed and plans put in place to maintain food supplies etc. That the Egyptians understood that the Sun, Moon and planets had an effect on all things in their world is now firmly appreciated and understood. Archaeology has brought us much information and knowledge of life in this area of our world. Egypt was not only powerful but also rich with gold from their neighbour countries especially Nubia, also they were rich in tributes from the various countries that they conquered. Egypt merits much investigation as I am sure that even now much more awaits to be revealed regarding the knowledge and capabilities of the Egyptian nation in those days.

When things like famines, floods that destroyed homes etc in the surrounding countries, many of those inhabitants fled to Egypt for comfort and support. Notably Abraham, Jacob, Joseph and of course Jesus himself who was taken there by Joseph his father.

Having established the importance of Egypt in those days I will now move on with the story of the enigmatic Moses. I have written in great detail on this character in one of my other books so I will keep to the brief and poignant details regarding him but must not diminish his importance within Freemasonry and to this book.

You will, I hope, remember the biblical story of MOSES in that the Pharoah at the time was seriously concerned over the proliferation of the Hebrews, in that they may become so large in number that they could rise up against him and actually succeed in a coup.

The prolific number of Hebrews that were said to be living in Egypt at this time seems incredible, but according to Rabbi Ken Spiro, the 70 individuals that arrived in Egypt at the time of Joseph, had grown to a nation of about 3 million. This is not as far-fetched as it may at first appear. If each family emulated Jacob, and went forth and multiplied, that is had twelve children, you can easily compute that in five generations there will be this many people, if not more. This seems incredible, but is distinctly possible and credible as ultra-orthodox Jewish families in Israel today follow a similar trend.

This apparent "rabbit-like" multiplication of the Hebrews made the Egyptians nervous – "there are too many of them, what if they rise up against us" – and the Pharaoh issues a genocidal decree: "Kill all the Jewish boys".

So he ordered the culling/killing of all Hebrew male children. At this juncture I must digress to discuss the power of the very strong maternal instinct. It is greatly appreciated that this natural instinct is so strong that mothers would fight to the death to protect their children. This is amply exemplified in the animal world. Ask any mother and they will confirm how powerful this natural instinct actually is. I implore that you keep this strongly in mind as we continue.

Moses, according to the Bible was born to Amram his father, a Levite and Jochebed his mother. He had 2 siblings, his brother Aaron who was 3 years older than him and a sister Miriam who was 7 years older.

When the order for the killing was issued Jochebed, his

mother, acted in a most peculiar manner. She immediately sent her daughter Miriam and her son Aaron to her husbands' Levite family where the Pharaoh's decree had no authority. OK, so she has fully protected her daughter and older son, but what of her son Moses? She protected him for 3 months hiding him as much as she could then as we read she placed him in a basket covered with pitch and sent him floating towards the palace of the Pharoah who ordered the killing of all the male children. This is not the instinctive action of a true mother. There must be reasons for this totally out of character action.

Sigmund Freud way back in 1929 wrote an excellent paper stating, and proving in his terms that Moses was in fact Egyptian and not from the Hebrew race. In our modern times Ahmed Osman has written a book along similar lines having the same conclusion.

Both give quite solid reasons produced from excellent research for this conclusion and as we progress with our own researches coupled with items from both these authorative writers, further evidence will likewise prove this conclusion that Moses the acknowledged founder of the Jewish religion, the leader and organiser of the Exodus was Egyptian and not as believed from the Hebrew race.

This conclusion sits most comfortably with Jochebed's action of placing baby Moses in a basket heading towards the Pharoah's palace. Further events that occurred at this time will further endorse this amazing conclusion.

Life in Egypt at this time was very male dominated. Women were very much second class citizens fit only for toil, physical pleasure, and domesticity. The Pharoah's word was law, if he said "jump" you literally asked "how high?".

The Pharoah's had three names, their birth name, their royal name and their godly name, as they were regarded as being next to God. For example Tutmoses, a very important godly name by reason of the suffix MOSES, means "Born of Thoth. Thoth was a very important God within the Egyptian pantheon of Gods (to whom I will be returning) as he holds an integral part in this research and explanation. Rameses, here I draw your attention again to the suffix, means "son of Ra", Ra being the Egyptian God of the Sun

Returning to the bible story we find that the Pharoah's daughter, a princess, goes down for her morning bathe and discovers the infant Moses in the basket, she then takes her find back to the palace, which is the house of the Pharoah who ordered the killings of every male child. How strange is this? She then tells the Pharoah, her father, that she is not only going to keep the child but will bring him up in the household of the very Pharoah who ordered his death, knowing he is a Hebrew.

Again quoting Rabbi Ken Spiro "The only modern equivalent would be of some fellow who is meant to overthrow Nazi Germany was raised as Adolf Hitler's adopted grandson......You realise what a wild story this is if you imagine it in a modern context." This is obviously an obfuscation for something else, or, as is constantly found, a metaphor for another actuality.

One other amazing aspect to this story is that Miriam, Moses's older sister, is portrayed as advising the princess how to bring up the infant. There is another logical explanation for these events. As in today, the elite of the populace used to hand their very young out to nursing or suckling mothers which would have naturally formed some sort of bond between the mother and child, also the mother's other children would have formed a certain bond. This explanation fits more logically with the bible story rather than the fanciful explanations we are regularly given. So if Jochebed was the suckling mother to (wet-nurse of) the child of the princess, her actions of sending her real children to safety and then protecting her suckling baby from the soldiers who would not know that the suckling was actually the son of a princess, she would have to release him back to his own mother. The logic of Miriam's involvement also fits into the logic of this explanation.

Moses's name in Hebrew means "saved from the water", obviously referring to being saved from the Nile after being placed there by Jochebed, and also being saved from the pursuing Egyptian army by the parting of the waters of the Red sea, how odd that he should be so named before both these events actually occurred.

So now we have more circumstances that bring serious doubt to Moses's actual origins.

For the next forty years of his life Moses was brought up within the palace of the Pharoah and according to the Bible "was taught all the wisdom of Egypt". This was amazing for a supposed adopted Hebrew child.

History shows that Moses was an incredible soldier, also that he learned everything regarding the Egyptian priesthood, part iof which would have been a complete appreciation of the God Thoth and all his workings and teachings.

Thoth was a very important Egyptian God, acclaimed to be the creator of all the sciences and the author of "The Egyptian Book of the Dead", He was also the "Judge of the Dead".

When an Egyptian died, his soul was said to be in limbo and appeared before Thoth and a number of lesser judges to answer a set of negative questions. Thoth had a set of scales which on one side had a feather and on the other the heart of the deceased. The negative replies of the questions took the form of negative statements:

1. *No, I have not taken the name of my God in vain.*
2. *No, I have not coveted my neighbours wife.*
3. *No, I have not fornicated.*
4. *No, I have not stolen or lied.*

And so on, and when sufficient correct answers were received the deceased's soul went up to join the Gods forever in peace. Now I will set a question to you, the reader. Where do you think Moses got his ideas for the 10 Commandments from? He would have been taught all about Thoth. These explained facts are gradually drawing us to the same conclusion as they did for Sigmund Freud and Ahmed Osman.

At the age of forty Moses came across an Egyptian soldier beating a Hebrew slave. He stepped in and prevented the beating going any further and so badly beat up the soldier that the soldier died immediately. The Hebrew slave had run off, and Moses looked around not seeing anyone else so quickly buried the soldier in the sand. Within a short while two slaves came up to him and told him that they witnessed the whole event and that they were prepared to reveal all. Moses apparently panicked and fled far away to Midian and became a shepherd.

This event is quite a puzzle in that life in Egypt was extremely cheap. Moses was so high up in the house of the Pharoah that he was regarded as being No 2 to the Pharoah. He could have easily, for no reason whatsoever, just being No.2 to the Pharoah, have ordered the soldier to be killed without any questions being asked. But he decided to flee. How odd was that? There is a distinct pattern of a changing of events in an attempt to make the creation of the Jewish nation a plausible and natural event. In this regard, there is an excellent book by Thomas Thompson called "The Bible" subtitled "How writers create a past". A very well written book well worthy of study. But back to Egypt and Moses.

Moses remained away from Egypt for another forty years, and during this time life continued in Egypt as it always did.

A Pharoah then inherited the Crown that had such an enormous impact on Egyptian life and religion that academics have speculated on for years. He was Amenhotep IV, son of Amenhotep III forming the 18th dynasty..

Amenhotep IV came to power with a plan. Egypt was fantastically wealthy at this time and Amenhotep IV decided that now was the time to instigate his plan. He decided that there would be just one supreme God, and that supreme God would be the Sun, or more correctly the power behind the sun. This was the beginning of monotheism, the worship of an all powerful, all knowing and ever present God. His belief was that you could only worship the one God and not share that devotion with any other Gods. There was no need for other Gods as his God was an all knowing, all powerful and ever present God and He made all other Gods unnecessary and superfluous. This took the populace some getting used to. Thousands of years of worshiping many Gods was difficult to undo and took time. The group that were most upset were those immediately put out of a job, namely the many priests supervising the worship of the many other Gods. The unrest caused meant that Amenhotep IV had to move somewhere else with his followers so that unimpeded worship could succeed and progress. He settled for El-Amarna and called the new city Akhentaten. The place of the Aten. Aten was the name for his God so the new city was the City of the Aten. Amenhotep IV then changed his name to AKHENATEN meaning "Son of the Aten, and the God Aten could only be reached through Akhenaten.

A complete construction of the city was made with a magnificent Temple dedicated to the Aten. The symbol of the Aten was a disc set in between two mountains and you will see this symbolic representation in the many Egyptian hieroglyphs.

Akhenaten married the beautiful Nefertiti and produced six daughters all named with a suffix of "Aten". Eventually a son was born whose name was Tutankhaten.

As time progressed the civic unrest, stirred up by the dislodged priests, plus Akhenaten's total lack of interest in the progress of Egypt overall led to what is supposed to be

Akhenaten   Nefertiti   Tutankhamun

his murder or assassination, and there are many academic theories on this very subject. His wife Nefertiti disappears, so his young son Tutankhaten is crowned as the Pharoah by the re-established priests. In time all reference to Akhenaten is removed from all walls, tombs and stelae.

When Tutankhaten grows up he is convinced by his "advisers" to change his name to Tutankamun, the suffix AMUN being a positive reference to the original Sun God. At the age of 18 Tutankamun changed his name back to Tutankhaten and started to revert back to his fathers ideas of a single God, but not for long. He too was murdered or assassinated and a new Pharoah was established and the old religious ways remain back in place. At this time many of the followers of the Aten left the city as they did not wish to go back to the old ways. Not much is written about this large group, as the Egyptians never wrote much regarding their failings, I say this but I may be entirely incorrect. Many serious academics including Sigmund Freud and Ahmed Osman believe, and there is much one could read supporting this, that Akhenaten was in actual fact Moses and his brother Aaron was his High Priest or perhaps the other way round, because of Moses's accepted Egyptian heritage and Aaron's Jewish heritage it is most likely that Moses was Akhenaten. Subsequently the many followers that left the city to continue their religion of a single God was in actual fact the biblical Exodus. Credible? Possibly. If you look at the Exodus as portrayed in the Bible, that number of people travelling in the desert for 40 years "until all the carcasses of that generation should have fallen in the wilderness", some trace, no matter how small would have been left somewhere. But despite the active interest and technological advances in archaeology not a single trace or chard has ever been found to prove this classically religious event.

In closing this long chapter on Egypt and Moses it is fully appreciated that Moses was never circumcised, which as we all know is a positive in Jewish culture, BUT his son Gershom was, simply in order for him to escape the angel of death during the Passover. How strange is all this?

What could it all mean. Questioning the written words in the Bible would normally be regarded as blasphemous or worse, heretical, but thankfully these days we are more aware, and better enlightened to know that the Bible has been edited at least eleven times since its first edition. Each edit being influenced first by Jewish scribes trying to create a past, culture and heritage for their new land of milk and honey and by the church elders to support their theories for their religion and dogma as they saw it, and then by many Rulers, Leaders including Henry the VIII in his opposition to the Pope, and lastly by King James, or on the order of him by William Schaw, a famous Freemason authorising its use as official.

There is one incident within the life of Moses that has always intrigued me the most and that is the story of the Burning Bush. The aspect of, and I quote is, "the bush that burns but is never consumed". Now we all know the consistent power of fire is that it ultimately consumes all that it burns, so this simple example of a flame that burns but does not consume takes an awful lot of faith in order to believe and fully accept.

I now have a reason for this aspect and an understanding of how it may have been created.

In that part of the world there is a bush known as the Acacia bush, which is different from the Acacia Tree. We know this plant as a Mimosa plant. In the Holy Land this plant has vivid orange flowers so that when the Sun beats down it appears that in the shimmering heat the bush is aflame but of course it is never actually burnt or consumed. This effect caused the local populace to refer to it in their dialect as "The Burning Bush". When the Greek Scribes many hundreds of years later were translating this item from the ancient Hebrew or Aramaic not realising or knowing of this plant they translated it literally. So now we have another apparent miracle.

Moses is very much revered throughout Masonic ritual and ceremonies, but his birth, the parting of the Red Sea, and many other miracle type aspects are not mentioned. There is a small part of a ceremony within a lecture that mentions part of that which occurred possibly in the Exodus but only to support some facts describing the actions of David the first King of Israel appointed by God.

Is the reason that those aspects could not be scientifically proven, or were far too fanciful to be used in explaining or endorsing moral and social principles in a more sophisticated society, or did our ancient Brethren actually know better. Our further readings could well assist in making those difficult decisions.

Archaeology today has come so far and so specialised, together with the aid of serious developing technology , and can now conclude many aspects that previously were no better than logical guesses.

By just a single tooth they can determine what the diet was of individuals at a particular period in history, they can also extract DNA and prove the hereditary origins of any race. These possibilities and a whole lot more are certainly causing us and others to take another look at history and its reasons. Here I will present just one example.

Intensely examining some Egyptian Mummies they have discovered the use of Cannabis and Cocaine. They have also proved that travel by reed boat from that part of the world to South America where the plants from which Cannabis and Cocaine are extracted were indigenous, in fact the only place at that time were indigenous.

These facts lead us to take a closer look at the culture of that area at the time in question. Their God Quetzalcoatl came from "out of the water", which means that he must have been a foreigner. He also sported a beard which, similar to the North American Indians, was something that the Mayan Indians and its neighbours found very difficult to do. Also in Egypt you can see The Broken Pyramid, The Bent Pyramid, The Ziggurats, all examples of the journey to finally building the perfect construction of the extremely difficult design of the actual pyramid. The Egyptian early mistakes can be seen and studied. In Meso-America there are no early mistakes, all their temples of varying design are all examples of Pyramidal perfection. How is this so with out outside assistance and guidance. It is not a huge leap of faith to assume that there must have been an exchange in the form of trade. Incredibly I have mentioned that numbers with their importance and meaning were of significance to the Egyptians and therefore the Jews as well, I discovered that some of the Mayan Temples had 72 steps leading up to the top area. Coupled with this the snake or serpent was so important to the cultures of Meso-America that sculptures of them were so placed on each side of the steps, that as the Sun ran its course the shadow of the serpents seemed to crawl up the steps.

The significance of the number 72 is well noted and explained within Freemasonry. In Egypt the serpent was always regarded as a symbol of wisdom and was constantly worn by the Pharaohs and made them "The Wise One". Moses had a sceptre with 2 serpents winding around it implying twice as wise. Even in our modern times this iconic symbol can be seen at most hospitals and pharmacies as if handed down from the ancient therapeutae. Aaron always carried a rod, and in the story of the time when he and Moses went to the Pharoah to obtain the release of the Hebrew peoples, the Pharoah then consulted with 7 of his sages who also had rods and who then threw them on the floor and they each turned into a serpent, which prompted Aaron to do likewise and his not only turned into a serpent but gobbled up the sages' seven serpents. This simply relates that Aaron's argument or wisdom was stronger than the Pharaohs sages. No magic or miracle implied. How else would you record this story to a people that could not read the written word but by pictogram. Again when translated centuries later by scribes that were used to the written word, it comes as no surprise for the mis-understanding.

So far many points have been made regarding the facts of the bible, Moses and Freemasonry, but we now have to investigate how all this progressed and became embedded as English and European Freemasonry. During this period from, Moses, faith and religion, and many other factors such as travel and trade continued to slowly gain momentum. Wars, minor and major took place. Empires rose and fell, but Faith remained the ultimate influence and from the first century onwards proved to be an even stronger element in separating or bringing together nations. In many areas across the then known world, the laws of the country was based on its religious laws thus causing many schisms within the respective faiths. In Christianity we now have Catholics, Protestants, Baptists, Lutherans etc. etc. In Judaism we have various types of the Jewish community, Sephardic, Hasmonean, Zealots, Essenic, Nasorean etc. etc. This schismatic feature occurs in many Faiths to a lesser or greater degree. The more people that are members of a faith the more diverse are the opinions of the understanding of that Faith. Some Faiths became so strong and powerful in their desire to be the foremost and in some cases the only Faith, that the cruellest atrocities were conducted by many in their attempts to achieve this. But our modern judgements must not be allowed to pollute what occurred in those distant dark days, for situations were very different as were people's attitudes. What was accepted then is certainly not accepted now, but History cannot, nor should it be, changed just to suit modern thinking and idealology. For good or for bad History remains what it is and was and should not be re-interpreted just to suit modernistic trends. With this in mind we will now seriously look at this enigmatic group known to us through history as THE KNIGHTS TEMPLAR.

CHAPTER 5
THE KNIGHTS TEMPLAR

Countless books, both fiction and those claiming to be fact have been, and will continue to be written about this enigmatic and mysterious group of knights known and revered as THE KNIGHTS TEMPLAR. They were originally known as "The Poor Fellow Soldiers of Christ" or, in their original language, Chevalier du Templair. I have, in one of my previous Masonic books written about this band of Brother Knights like so many others, but I have the distinction of being a Freemason and a member of the Masonic Knights Templar and so I am able to positively better make the necessary connections to prove my theory that Freemasonry was brought from the East through the offices of the Knights Templar.

Late in the 11th century 9 Knights, who were in most cases, related to each other and appear to have had some information, handed down within their related families, that led them to believe that there was some secret treasure or special knowledge awaiting discovery at the Temple of Solomon in Jerusalem. So for want of a communal meeting place, they began meeting in each other's houses on a fairly regular basis to discuss plans for a journey to the Holy Land, as it was their uncle Baldwin I who was the current King of Jerusalem at that time.

The meetings were fairly frequent and the local populace labelled them "House Brothers" which in Gallic French is" Frere Maison". This is no more great a leap of faith to go from Frere Maison to Free Mason, than those bible stories or other myths on which the most powerful faiths of the world are based. Re-think "Virgin births, curing blindness and leprosy, raising the dead etc. etc. Let us continue.

In the year 1099, nine Knights from Gaul, led by Godfrey de Bouillon entered Jerusalem, and beseeched King Baldwin I to convince him to allow them to reside in the Temple grounds. It was in the Temple stables that they made their base.There is positive archaeological proof that these knights tunnelled underneath the centre of the temple and possibly up into the level just below the Sanctum Sanctorum or most sacred place. They must have discovered something, and there are many legends speculating on what actually was found, because subsequently Hugh de Payens petitioned Baldwin II who inherited the crown of jerusalem, for permission for these nine knights to establish themselves as a new religious order. This permission was granted. They changed the name from "The Poor Fellow Soldiers of Christ" and became the Knights Templar. They became known by many titles, but were popularly remembered as Knights Templar. For the next nine years little is recorded of their actions. Neither did they take in any new recruits, which is rather strange for a new order. As I have mentioned all these nine knights came from Champagne in Gaul, and most were closely related in some way. They were originally thought to be protecting pilgrims on their way to the Holy Land, but there is no actual records of them doing this. This appears to be a guise for whatever their actual purpose was.

These Knights must have discovered something which I think was some special nowledge and not actual treasure or religious artifacts.

So, Hugh de Payens had left Jerusalem as one of a small group of an obscure unofficial order, returning just two years later with 3oo knights, the backing of the Pope and many of the kings of Europe, and untold wealth and land.

Knights Templar

During this two year absence, they petitioned the Pope for the official backing of the Roman Catholic church with all the power that it entailed. They must have revealed something of what they discovered, and I doubt if it was any of the particular religious artifacts so often speculated on.

Religious artifacts were big business in those days. The display of whatever artifact was conducted would bring thousands of pilgrims to the church which would also bring offerings and monies. So if the Ark of the Covenant, The Holy Grail, the 10 Commandments, or any of the many objects that are regularly speculated upon, rest assured they would be amply displayed in order to attract aspirants into the faith and money into their coffers. As this has never happened we must assume that there are no such artificats to display. So the conclusion must be that they found some knowledge that would have great impact on Christianity especially if it were revealed, because they were granted complete backing of the most powerful faith at that time coupled with extra privileges such as tax exemption etc. A very powerful position to be in!!

Through Bernard of Clairvaux, nephew to one of the nine and Abbott of the Cistercian Order, and later to be canonised as St.Bernard, they obtained a Rule from the Pope. With this powerful religious backing of the Pope and the Holy Roman Catholic Church, Bernard of Clairvaux, known as the "Second Pope", and King Baldwin II of Jerusalem, they were now officially formed and recognised as such. They were not originally set up as an Order of Chivalry, but primarily as an escort of protection for the pilgrims making their way to the Holy Land. Whereas the Hospitallers or Knights of St.John were formed to administer aid and succour to those pilgrims who fell foul to the many bandits on their route.

Bernard championed their cause vociferously and urged that they be supported with gifts of land and money and encouraged aristocratic young men to forget their sinful lives and take up the sword and the cross as Templar Knights. So successful was his canvassing that the King of France gave both monies and substantial grants of land, which was promptly followed by similar gestures from others of the nobility. King Stephen of England did likewise. The knights were granted many productive manors which provided a continuous income.

Over the next 200 years they were to become the most powerful and respected force in the then known world. With all this support of land and monies together with expert and diverse internal management, the Knights Templar became possibly the first conglomerate organisation in the world.

Over the years they expanded to have a Fighting Arm, a Maritime Arm, A Business Arm, a Legal Arm and a Building Arm. This building Arm was known as "The Children of Solomon". They built preceptories and castles all over Europe and the Middle East also many beautiful Cathedrals such as Notre Dame, Chartres, many of which still stand today. They also built up a tremendous fleet of ships, and conducted trade with spices and silks etc. Their fighting prowess was justifiably legendary. They were also skilled in commerce, law and financial matters, holding the treasuries of both England and France. Many European kings were in their financial debt, especially King Phillip of France. They were considered experts in law and helped to structure the legal system of England at the time. Their main preceptory, and the surrounding area known as Temple Bar, in London, is still steeped in the legal profession.

I could go into their successes and failures whilst in the Holy Land but as this book is really about the connection of Freemasonry and the Knights Templar, I will leave their successes and failures to the many other books that exist on this subject.

At their zenith of power and wealth, as is always the case, envy became the bed for malicious gossip and rumour. Their secret rites, initiations and ceremonies were speculated to be blasphemous. Phillip le Bel, King of France saw this as an opportunity to grab their wealth and power, and therefore automatically absolve himself of his huge financial debt to them, he conspired with the Pope, whom history proves was in actual fact his puppet, to 'annihilate' the Order on charges of heresy. To all of which the Pope agreed. This was effected in absolute secrecy, so that on Friday the 13th October 1307, 5,000 Knights Templar were arrested and imprisoned in France. This date (Friday the 13th) has held fear and dread for many people ever since although the origins have become lost in the mist of time.

When, however, the arresting soldiers went to take charge of their the Templar fleet of ships in La Rochelle, it had gone, together with the Templar treasury, so the secrecy could not have been as absolute as was believed. The Pope insisted that the regents of the other European countries should activate his ruling in the same way. But most at first refused, finding the accusations unbelievable of for such a revered order. This delay gave the overseas based knights the time to regroup and make plans for their escape accordingly. The arrested knights, in France, were subjected to the most excruciating torture, and many falsely confessed, under these conditions, to the charges of heresy, and were subsequently burned. Many died faithful to the principals of the Order. Even the Grand Master, Jacques de Molay, confessed under torture, but recanted his confession, along with the Treasurer of the Order, before meeting their death from burning.

This whole process from arrest until the death of the Grand Master took nearly seven years, and there are many authoritative books available on this subject, giving great detail of all the events. The other main countries handled this situation very differently. In Portugal the Knights Templar disbanded and formed The Knights of Christ, and continued under that banner. In Germany they joined up with the Teutonic Knights, some even joined the Knights Hospitaller of St. John, or as they became known The Knights of Malta, who are the inspiration behind our own St.Johns Ambulance Brigade, who have as their insignia the 8 pointed cross of the ancient Order.

The Pope then gave a decree that the Knights Templar were should be formally disbanded, and declared that all their wealth and land acquisitions be handed over to the Knights Hospitaller, after having taken some for the Holy See as administrative costs, likewise the King of France. The Knights Hospitaller, rather than standing by their brother knights, eagerly grabbed this opportunity of swelling their own ranks, wealth and power. A fact that the fugitive Knights Templar never forgot. As I have mentioned before, there are many authoritative books on this subject each with their own theories and explanations, some very far-fetched and some more realistic.

You must appreciate that the religion dominant at this time, the Holy Roman Catholic Church, was all-powerful, superior in power even, to many European Kings. And totally used this power in any way they saw fit to procure the subjection of its pan-European? congregation, and to further strengthen its own hold and power. Anyone who spoke out against the workings of the "Church" was duly deemed a heretic and put to the stake. Therefore people were genuinely in fear of their lives, and having witnessed, over a few short years, the total obliteration of a once omnipotent knightly order, felt total justification for their fear and dread.

I said "totally obliterated", but was it actually ?

We must now look at what could have happened to those knights that appear to have fled !!

First we must look at the Fleet of the Knights Templar and the treasure, whatever that was. As I mentioned earlier they must have had prior knowledge of their impending doom for their ships were nowhere to be found. The main fleet containing the treasure found its way to Scotland. A land with its own problems, being ex-communicated as a country, by the Church of Rome; therefore the Papal Bull against the Templars was never sent to Scotland, and consequently was non-effective, thereby making it an ideal haven for the fleeing fugitives.

There was also strife within the nation itself over its sovereignty, and it was constantly at loggerheads with England. One of the prominent senior family groups of the Knights Templar through its inception and progression was the original Gallic noble family called St.Clair. This family formed a stronghold in Scotland and became the Sinclairs, who throughout the centuries have held prominence with Scottish nobility and higher government, even to this very day, being very well recorded in Scottish history and many recent books, especially those on the Chapel at Rosslyn, which was built by the Sinclairs, and is believed to hold a very strong Masonic influence.

Some of the fleet continued to sail the seven seas preying on the ships of the very Catholic countries they felt were responsible for their demise. These ships were manned by "pirates and corsairs", a phrase I would ask you to bear in mind., and now I Lacking a national flag, they sailed under the banner of a very well known symbol of the Templars, which has become an important symbol within Freemasonry, and I mean the "Skull and Crossbones". This sigil is to be found on many Templar graves, especially in Scotland, as it was the way many of them were buried. A tradition that seems to be borrowed from the Jewish method of having the bones of the deceased placed in a stone ossuary box.

A very successful captain of one of these ships was Sir Roger de Monfort, and his "ensign" became known as "The Jolly Roger", a title now synonymous with Pirates of whatever stripe.

Bearing in mind the delay on the part of the English King to implement the Papal Bull against the Knights Templar, this would have afforded the persecuted knights time to re-group and receive the news that their fleet and many of their brothers in arms had found a safe haven in Scotland. They would have needed to travel there under cover, which of course was no real problem for they were quite used to developing passwords, codes and all the necessary subterfuge for fugitives on the run from their experience of delicate and secretive financial dealings.

It is somewhat strange how words originally designed for a "cloak and dagger" purpose become absorbed into modern vocabulary without many realising its true origin. One of these words is "ROSE" as in the ceiling rose, through which we hang our central light - why not a tulip or dandelion, why a "ROSE" ? I will digress and explain.

There was an old system called in Latin "SUB-ROSA" meaning "under the rose" The ancient Romans used to hang roses, particularly white roses over their dining tables to signify that anything said under the roses was deemed safe and never to be quoted outside. In the Middle Ages houses used to surround their doorways with white roses to signify that this was a sympathetic household or a "safe house. The Victorians would make plaster emblems of roses and stick them in the centre of their ceilings over the dining table to signify confidence and freedom in after dinner conversation. With the advent of gas and electricity being placed in the centre of the room, the pipework or wire was passed through the middle of "The Rose", and the name has continued ever since although many do not realise its origins , age or significance.

This type of sign would have been second nature to their particular system of secrecy, which had been finely honed over the past 200 years. They developed a system of "safe houses" and collaborators throughout England leading, by various routes up to Scotland. Where they were welcomed for their various skills and possibly most of all for their undoubtable battle tactics and fighting skills, as the conflagrations between Scotland and England were now coming to a head.

We should now look at the Battle of Bannockburn and Robert the Bruce. Legend has it that Bruce herded all the elderly folk, women and children to drape white sheets over their heads and at the strategically given signal, to come charging and screaming over the hill and hopefully scare the English Army into retreat. According to romantic legend this is what happened, and the ruse did put the whole English Army to flight!

Romantic ? Yes. Realistic ? No ! The more likely scenario is that after agreeing certain terms with Robert the Bruce on a victory at Bannockburn, the fugitive Knights Templar agreed to advise and assist him in his plight, being heavily outnumbered by the English Army.

Agreement was obviously reached for at the most strategic moment of the battle the Knights Templar led a fearsome decisive charge towards the ranks of the English Army. The sight of such a fearsome force in their white mantles together with their famous battle-cry "Beau Seant", meaning "be noble", or "be glorious", charging full pelt on their famous war horses, with their fearsome reputation going before them is what put the fear of God into the

Robert the Bruce

English Army. And they did indeed flee, pursued by the jubilant Scots, who immediately slew all they caught. (As an aside there is an interesting fact in a poem by the Scottish Poet Laureate Robbie Burns, an acknowledged Freemason, in his poem about a Crofter and his sheep dog, he remarks on the dogs "Bawsant" face, meaning his black and white face. The Beau Sant flag of the Knights was half black and half white. Now just where did this word used by Robbie Burns originally come from?

This incident is the main reason for the success of the Scots at Bannockburn. It is historically recorded that at

Bannockburn, immediately after the victory Robert the Bruce founded the first Lodge of Kilwinning, and I quote, ".....for the reception of those Knights Templar who had fled from France...." This obviously was part of the Templar deal with him.

Many scholarly historians have attributed the rise of Freemasonry in this manner.

In those days of fanatical religious persecution where there were dire consequences for anyone who hinted at the possibility of being even slightly heretic, the need for anyone fully accused of such a crime, whether true or false, to flee and go underground, was paramount, if you wanted to survive. And the Templars wanted to survive in some form or another.

As the Knights Templar, throughout their formidable history, through the efforts of their building arm The Children of Solomon, were entirely steeped in the building of many, many marvellous cathedrals, castles and churches, the construction of which still amaze the architects of today, plus their own culture, with which they became embroiled over the centuries, would naturally be influenced by any ascetic/esoteric knowledge they may acquire, from the many cultures and schisms they encountered on their many travels, particularly in the Middle East. The most sensible candidate for an expression of their precepts would have to be one that they were already very familiar with, and that candidate was the art of building, or MASONRY. Like a river which begins at the top of a mountain, pure and unsullied, and, on its travels to its final destination, becomes infiltrated many times, sometimes enhanced and sometimes polluted, or even changed off its course, but inevitably its journey must cause change, however slight, from its pure beginnings. Templarism cannot be excluded from this analogy. For example, the religious persecution brought about the biggest change to Templarism, whilst it was on its metaphoric journey. It forced its change to masonry. As, up until that time, Templarism had built as a shield to its possible actualities, the outward image of "Warrior Monks", and I personally have no doubt that this was in reality just a shield for whatever their real purpose might have been, for there is no record of them having actually protected pilgrims on the road to the Holy Land, which if you remember was their original supposed "raison d'etre". But they were warrior monks for most of their existence in the Holy Land So the Templars were quite used to this sort of subterfuge, and to slide into another "shield" more suitable to the times than warrior monks, would have been relatively simple for them, and to me quite obvious.

Before closing this particular chapter I would just like to go back to the building arm of the Templars namely the Children of Solomon. Naturally the soldier knights did the fighting as the sailor knights took care of the maritime business etc,. etc.The Children of Solomon were Master builders and Sculptors, their skills being appreciated and admired in such buildings as Notre Dame and Chartres Cathedral, both of which contain much masonic symbolism among other things.

Having decreed that the Knights Templar were heretics receiving the penalties deserving of this crime, the Pope also decreed that the Children of Solomon, having erected such beautiful buildings to the Glory of God, were to be absolved of any heretical crimes and were allowed to go free.

It would come as no surprise to me to learn that some important senior knights claimed to be members of The Children of Solomon, so that they could go free to maintain there knightly society secretly elsewhere and come out of hiding once it was safe to do so, no matter how long it took. Appreciating how long it took to build up such a powerful organisation there was no way were they going to allow it to disappear for ever.

Furthermore some knights fled over the Alps and in time assisted in bringing together several sovereignties to form the country we now know as Switzerland. Look at the culture of Switzerland and its banking practise of secret codes and numbered accounts. Look at the flag of Switzerlend and compare it to the symbol of the Knights Templar, one is a mirror image of the other. One of the early codes of the Knights Templar was mirror-imaging. This is duly noted and supported by many academics, in particular Daniel Dafoe the Canadian Historic author.

CHAPTER 6

FREEMASONRY AND THE TEMPLARS

Thus, in 1314 ended this official historic order known as the Knights Templar.

This ends the thumbnail history of the Knights Templar, and now would be a good time to bring in some of the Templar "icons" to be found in Freemasonry today. It must be borne in mind that the whole organisation was a vast conglomerate importantly needed to run the various "arms" of the business, and their trade in the various goods like silks and spices would have brought them closely in touch with several cultures and religions throughout their sphere of travel. Any corporate business involved in many diverse fields must be aware of its customer needs even if they do not personally subscribe to their particular beliefs. But naturally aspects would "rub off" on to them and the many aspects that did would culminate possibly in an adjustment to their thinking. But the absolute power of religion and the Church would force them not to reveal these changes until they felt the possibility of the threat of "heresy" and its inevitable punishments was no longer in existence.

Looking back at the charges of heresy made against the Knights Templar, one of the most serious was that they "trampled on the cross of Christ". The reality of the actual step that they took was exactly the same action made by Freemasons in the step that they take during the various ceremonies..

To the Knights it represented the actual " T " bar cross now accepted by most biblical scholars to be the actual style of the true cross of Jesus, and not the artistic traditional style with the extended upright. When translated to Masonic symbolism this step represents the " Tau " cross, said to be the most perfect figure in geometry, and represented on the Installed Masters Apron, indicating that three steps have been completed, and also has importance in other degrees in Freemasonry. We must remember that in transferring from Templarism to Masonry, they also, in the process, de-Christianised most of their symbolism, something they had to do in those fanatically Catholic dominated times. This simple transfer of symbolic representation loses nothing of its importance or impact if rightly understood. Most of the symbolic penalties of Freemasonry represent to "those with eyes to see", the sort of tortures that their comrades the Knights Templar were subjected to, during the persecution. One of the extreme penalties suffered by those that refused to submit to the charges of heresy, was that of being hanged until almost dead, the gut being slightly opened, and the entrails pulled out and burned while the victim was forced to watch. When finally dead from being "Hung and Drawn", the body was cut into four pieces and put on spikes to be displayed in the four corners of the city as a warning to others. Thus "Hung, Drawn and Quartered", It doesn't take a lot of imagination to see the hidden similarities of the 3rd degree, the four corners of the city being represented by the four Cardinal Winds of Heaven. The Templar Initiation ceremony and progression was similarly effected by degrees, as the aspirant progressed, more was revealed, after a test of merit. The one thing that finally clinched it for me was the names of some of the "Officers", and the one that takes the prize is the name of the officer who stood outside the door of their preceptory, being armed with a drawn sword, and was called in old Gallic, "Le Tailleur" (pron. Tye-er). Meaning, "He who cuts". Nowhere else have I seen a more sensible origin for this very important office, and believe me there have been many suggested.

It has been hinted by many eminent historians that there was an organising force behind the peasants revolt. Even Winston Churchill in his History of the English speaking people (italics), mentions the significance of a Great Society behind it. It does seem incredible to me that an insignificant illiterate peasant can rise from nowhere, and for eight weeks command, control and organise up to a 100,000 peasants to form an incredible rebellion.The logistics involved in doing this today would be quite phenomenal, but in those days with no phone, fax, or any communication other than personal contact, it would appear nigh on impossible, certainly beyond the capabilities of a mere peasant. It is now realised that the majority of the buildings that the peasants destroyed were the Catholic churches and residences of the Knights Hospitaller. The Templar properties were left intact. How were the peasants able to make this distinction!! The two most important people that were beheaded by the peasants' apparent anarchy, were the Archbishop of Canterbury, head of the Roman Catholic Church in England, and the Grand Master of the Knights Hospitaller. Why were these two so special to the peasants? Could it be that in exchange for assistance, organisation, and a system of secret codes, from the fugitive Knights Templar, a promise of revenge was carried out by the two leaders of the revolt, the most significant one being called Walter the "Tyler"- just where do you think he got his title from ?

The word Cowan is very interesting and was first introduced in Old Scottish Masonry to describe a person who could do the work of a stonemason but did not possess the Mason's Word, and has often been used by masonic writers to prove the link to the Guilds, as this word is used by the guilds to describe an unqualified craftsman, or non Guild member trying to practice the artisan craft. But I am afraid, in my opinion, they are wrong. A careful perusal of the "Old Charges" reveals the qualifications for acceptance into a Masonic Lodge, the applicant must be free born of a free mother, without physical impediment, sane, and not in his nonage or dotage, that is to say not too young or too old. For if you think about it, how could you, under the religious persecution ruling at that time, being a fugitive, fully trust someone who was not quite all there, through their lack of common sense, or being crippled in some way, or through being too young or too old. the latter two being covered by the words nonage and dotage.

In old Gallic there is a word "COUENNE" (pron. KOO-WAHN), which means "ignoramus" or "bumpkin", aptly describing just the sort of person to whom you would be most unwise to trust your secrets, least of all possibly your very life. It makes profound sense, if you are a group of fugitives, on the run from fear of religious persecution, to have an armed guard outside your door to keep off idiots and snoopers.

In one of the degrees of modern Freemasonry the aspirant is informed that this degree will make him a brother to "Pirates and Corsairs", I ask you, what does a pirate or a corsair have to do with a stonemason, it can only refer to the fate of some of the fleeing Knights Templar (such as Sir Roger de Monfort), and to be a constant reminder of those that took to the high seas to escape the persecution.

The toast to Absent Brethren is self explanatory.

The toast to "poor and distressed freemasons where're dispersed over the face of earth and water", can only refer to the scattered Knights Templar, and, in the hope that the religious persecutions end...."wishing them a safe return to their native land, should they so desire"...fairly self-explanatory !!!

The Knights Templar used to wear white lambskin "drawers" under their mantles as a sign of purity, and try as I did I could find no evidence of the operative masons wearing white lambskin aprons, they wore aprons made from rough cloth or ordinary cowhide but not white lambskin. Also I could find no actual evidence of ancient stonemasons wearing white gloves. But according to ancient manuscripts the Knights Templar wore white gloves to preserve their hands for when they "touched God".

NPIn the degrees of Craft Freemasonery there are Tracing Boards that contain much symbolism which is explained within the respective lectures that are givren during the relative degree. In the Master Mason degree there is a lecture on the Third Degree Tracing Board. On this Board there is a secret Masonic code, that very few Freemasons ever realise. Part of this code contains come characters that when translated form a specific date that when read correctly appear in "Mirror-image", one of the early codes of the Knights Templar.

Lastly, the obvious fact that the ceremonies revolve around their first and main objective The Temple of Solomon. To crown this explanation of the origins of Freemasonry, there is a very popular order in Freemasonry that does confirm that Freemasonry did emanate from the Knights Templar, but does not quote any of the reasons of proof that I have offered here, it just simply states it as a fact.

Bearing in mind, and if you accept the facts previously given, the Knights Templar now having achieved some sort of revenge for their terrible persecution, with the deaths of the Catholic Archbishop of Canterbury, and possibly avenged the death of their own Grand Master, Jacques de

Molay with the death of the Grand Master of the Knights Hospitaller, they were now able to carry on their pursuits, albeit under an apparently different guise, and to quietly watch the developments evolving, and therefore pick the appropriate time for revelation, as and when they saw fit.

Bearing in mind that the accepted Mother Grand Lodge of Freemasonry has been, and still is, the respected head of Freemasonry world-wide, it makes a great deal of sense to maintain our researches into Freemasonry and the Knights Templar within the history of England, which I will now do.

Having brought us from 1099 to about 1385 with the Knights Templar, you may well ask "Why did they wait until 1717 to come out of the closet, another 330 years?" A good question, which I will briefly answer. You must bear in mind that England was still a very staunch Catholic country, influenced strongly by the Roman Catholic Church, so it was extreme folly and potentially life threatening to reveal any other religious beliefs, no matter how tenuous. The threat of heresy and its retribution was very real.

But soon the wheels of change would slowly begin to move and change begin, as I will now explain with a brief overview of the events leading up to 1717.

Most of the 15th Century passed with little historic change. According to ancient manuscripts "Masonry" was steadily growing, and attracted many great thinkers of the times.

On 22/8/1485 King Richard III lost the throne and his life at the Battle of Bosworth to Henry Tudor, the Welsh Earl of Richmond, who married Elizabeth of York. His eldest son Arthur died in 1502 from T.B. The next son Henry, aged 18, succeeded in 1509, as Henry the VIII, and married the widow Catharine of Aragon within 6 weeks. After many failed births, in 1516 a daughter, Mary, was finally born. Henry then married Anne Boleyn and sired Elizabeth.

Henry was very belligerent and self centred, and caused many rifts and arguments with the Roman Catholic Church and its staunch followers. He did not take kindly to being directed by someone from abroad who was not even a King. So he then formed the Anglican Catholic Church, amid great unrest and general civic dissension against the Roman Catholic Church, due once again to their stern rules and continuing acquisition of wealth, power and especially land.

Edward VI was crowned in 1547 aged 10, ruling for 6 years, and under the guidance of his "advisers", repealed the laws of heresy and thereby opened the doors for Protestantism.

Lady Jane Grey, backed by a" Non-Catholic group", took the throne over Mary, who was a staunch Catholic, and ruled for nine days. Mary then ousted her and ruled for five years, as a fierce Catholic, being ferocious in her faith and its implementation, ordering 300 executions in 3 years. This ferocious campaign increased the religious bitterness already prevalent among her subjects. She went down in history as "Bloody Mary".

Elizabeth, influenced by her" close associates" when queen, re-instated her fathers Anti-Church laws and was ultimately ex-communicated by the Pope. Under Elizabeth England moved more towards Protestantism, some going even further and creating "Puritanism".

1603 saw the death of Elizabeth and the succession of James VI of Scotland as England's James I. The country was in such religious turmoil, which ultimately led to civil war. There were many assassination plots. The most famous attempt by Guy Fawkes. We still celebrate this failed attempt on November the 5th, but few people today realise that the effigy burned on the fire was originally that of the Pope and not, as it is supposed today, of Guy Fawkes. Such was the level of anti-Catholic feeling.

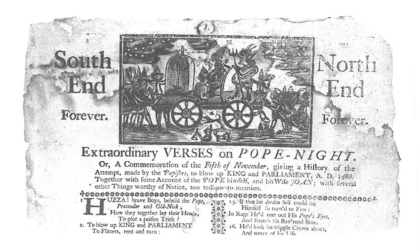

Extraordinary VERSES on *POPE-NIGHT.*

Or, A Commemoration of the *Fifth of November*, giving a History of the Attempt, made by the *Papishes*, to blow up KING and PARLIAMENT, A. D. 1588. Together with some Account of the *POPE* himself, and his Wife *JOAN*; with several other Things worthy of Notice, too tedious to mention.

1. HUZZA! brave Boys, behold the Pope, Pretender and Old-Nick; How they together lay their Heads, To plot a poison Trick?
2. To blow up KING and PARLIAMENT To Flitters, rent and torn;

15. If that his *derden* Self could see Himself so turn'd to Fun: In Rage He'd tear out His *Pope's Eyes*, And scratch his Rev'rend Bum.
16. He'd kick his tripple Crown about, And weary of his Life.

James I's greatest achievement was the King James Bible, which is still the biggest selling book today. This was achieved through his close friend and mentor William Shaw, who is the same individual responsible for the Shaw manuscripts, famous in Freemasonry, and which influences most of our rituals.

James died in 1625 and was succeeded by Charles I. Throughout his reign religious unrest increased even further, until in 1642 Civil War broke out with Charles and the Church on one side and The House of Commons with Oliver Cromwell on the other. It is interesting to note, at this juncture, that there are many quoted incidents regarding the "Freemasons" of both sides, the most distinctive being, that although a Puritanist, Cromwell was also a Freemason, and when his army entered Scotland to rout the Catholics and High Anglican Church followers, although they burned and sacked Rosslyn Manor, they did not touch the famous Chapel in any way shape or form. They razed the manor to the ground but left Rosslyn Chapel, with all its Masonic iconography unscathed. Something totally out of character for their religious beliefs but obviously not for their stronger Masonic ones.

Charles was defeated in 1642 and on January 30th 1649 he was beheaded.

Cromwell as Protector was too puritanical and dictatorial and died in September 1658, his son was too ineffective and the Army invited Charles II to take the throne. On 29th May 1660 Charles came home. In 1666 the Great Fire of London occurred.

The existence of Freemasonry is well documented during Charles II reign and during James II it grew even more, but James was a Catholic. The "Protestant leaders" invited Mary and William of Orange, both strong Protestants, to take the throne.

In 1701 a law was passed allowing only members of the Church of England to take the throne, thereby precluding any future Catholic monarch. This law is still in force today. Also in 1701, Anne, daughter of James II, and the last of the Stuarts, being a staunch Protestant, became Queen.

In 1707 the Union between Scotland and England joined their two crowns and "Great Britain" was born.

In 1714 Anne died and George I began the Hanoverian Dynasty. The country was ruled by Government and strictly Protestant.

In 1715 the Jacobite rebellion surfaced and was quickly put down.

There have, over the centuries, been many accusations that Freemasonry has been quietly instrumental in instigating changes in governmental law and statutes, changes in social reform etc. etc. Even have they been hinted at being the power behind the throne. Noting the comments of Churchill, mentioned earlier regarding the Peasants' Revolt, and the apparent influence of the advisers, and also the influences in other areas such as the Non-Catholic group, Protestant leaders etc. Plus the relationship of William Shaw and King James. The same for the Templars and eventually the Sinclairs and Scotland. The final Union of Scotland and England. We must also bear in mind that one of the main and possibly most laudable of Freemasonrys' principles is to bring about, by the most peaceful means of democracy and understanding, a better world for all, and in no way can it be professed to be a world takeover or domination as is oft times proclaimed. It is difficult not to draw the obvious conclusions.

So ended the centuries long failed struggle to return England to Catholicism and the Holy Roman Church.

With the power of the Roman Catholic Church and its dominant Catholicism removed, now it was safe for the "Knights Templar" to come out of hiding. As Scotland, being ex-communicated, was attractive to the fugitive Knights Templar, so England, with the death of dominant Catholicism, was now attractive to the Knights Templars' new image of "FREEMASONRY" !!!

Two years later, in 1717, 4 Masonic Lodges decided to "come out of the closet", now that they had no further need for secrecy, and no reason to hide from the establishment and established plans for the Premier Grand Lodge of Freemasonry.

CHAPTER 7
IN CONCLUSION

The conclusion of this book is wholly and purely my own personal opinion based on many years of diligent researches and investigations. The many books that I have read on this subject have offered a little insight into explaining some of the aspects I have raised but the biggest input has proved to be my actual involvement as a Freemason and in joining the many different Masonic Orders that are involved in this wonderful system.

Many notable scholars have written some excellent books on the subject of Freemasonry and its origins, but those that were not actual Freemasons have failed to connect all the links. One author whom I know wrote an excellent book on the Templars was John Robinson author of "Born in Blood". John was a Professor of Medieval history at a Chicageo University. At the time of his writing he was not a Freemason but became one soon after, obviously because of what he ultimately discovered.

In reality as romantic as the idea that Freemasonry came from the artisan trade of building may be it has very little that one could possibly state that as a fact, the same must apply to the Guilds. Both are laudable fraternities and societies with similar aspirations as that of Freemasonry, but again failing to complete the links necessary for a definitive conclusion.

Freemasonry, like many other institutions did not suddenly appear, it is far too complex for such a conclusion. It evolved over the millenia much like faith or religion. It is my contention that the Knights Templar having spent 200 years in the Holy Land, had involved themselves in the faiths and cultures of those times, in order to gain understanding of whom they were living, fighting and trading with and much of those faiths and cultures would have rubbed off on to them finally giving them a slightly different appreciation of the accepted religious Christian stories. Whatever knowledge they did actually discover none of us really knows, but events show that it must have been quite substantial to encourage the Pope to grant their wishes and to lending the Papacy's powerful support to the 'Templar Project'. Maybe the "Treasure" they discovered was information that made them think again about the manner in which their faith was being conducted, but as the Pope etc., were their backers it could not be fully revealed until circumstances proved to be the right time for such a revelation. During the time of Enlightenment when many established intelligent men like Sir Isaac Newton, Sir Christopher Wren, Elias Ashmole et al became involved via the Invisible College and later the Royal Society who knows what these great thinkers of science actually achieved within the society of Freemasonry that we have today.

Quite recently something occurred that we now know as a fact in that Dr. Barbara Frale an Italian palaeographer at the Vatican Secret Archives discovered an ancient parchment behind a cabinet. This parchment decreed that the Knights Templar were decreed by the Pope to be totally absolved from all charges of heresy. This parchment is dated August 1308 and must have been "suffocated" possibly on the orders of King Phillip le Bel . So, "sliding" into the Children of Solomon" in order to survive and secretly maintain their ultimate objectives, were all that the senior Knights could do as they were denied, once again, the chance of realistic freedom.

The Church, mainly the Catholic Church, has historically maintained an abhorrence towards Freemasonry, and this abhorrence has never been fully understood as, in reality there is nothing incompatible with any faith or belief system within the teachings of Freemasonry, but may be, and it is a may be, that the Templars did bring back some sacred knowledge that would have really shaken up the church's teachings and dogma thereby making their existence much less essential than they profess it to be.

Throughout history the Catholic Church has traditionally violently opposed anything contrary to their teachings, especially the developments of science and archaeology. It is still preaching the same dogma it has developed from the Bible Gospels in the same manner that it did in the beginning, even though knowledge within its congregation has progressed through science and understanding. Unless the Church grows with its congregation and shares the knowledge that life in general produces its existence will continue to stagnate. I believe there is nothing wrong with Faith or Religion or any belief system for that matter, as long as it grows and develops with modernity in all its forms.

I really wish that I could state positively that my conclusions are firmly correct, alternatively I cannot state that my conclusions are not correct, and in fact no one can not even the United Grand Lodge of England, so therefore the answer is basically up for grabs. The best that anyone can actually do is to take what lies comfortable with them, and what assists in them enjoying what they might be involved with. Thanking you for reading what lies comfortable for me. Whether you agree or disagree I trust that you enjoyed the journey.

Ray Hudson
September 2020.

NOTES ON THE ATTACHED PAPER
CONCERNING
THE ORDER OF SAINT SOPHIA

Having completed the whole manuscript for this book, I sent it to a good friend for his opinion on it and its conclusions. After a short period of time he sent me a paper that he had received from a very close friend of his, but from loyalty to his friend he was unable to reveal the name of the author of the paper. The paper lent a great deal of support to my researches and, I might say, to the possibility of my conclusions not being far away from realistic possibility, as it detailed similar connections elsewhere, and as the authority with which it was written, the author must have had some inside knowledge or at the very least a very close connection.

I felt compelled to beseech my friend if I could include the paper in my book with a full accreditation to its author. I was overjoyed to hear him say that he would pursue the request to the authors wife, as the author, his close friend had passed away recently.

After a period of time he came back to me with the wonderful news that the author's wife was happy to give the permission on behalf of her late husband on the premise that his great work should be appreciated and made available to the wider audience, and she agreed that my book would be a good place for its publication.

So, it is with the greatest of pleasure and the utmost respect that I can reveal that the author was none other than John, Baron von Hoff !, a very senior Freemason, yes, the precise same family that is constantly referred to in his paper, so without any doubts this paper must come with the greatest *gravitas* that any researcher, like myself, could ever wish for.

My sincere thanks, in a like manner, go to Pauline, Baroness von Hoff who, on her husband's behalf gave the hoped for permission for the publication.

Read and enjoy this wonderful and detailed paper.

Ray Hudson
December 2020.

THE ORDER OF SAINT SOPHIA
(HOLY WISDOM),
AND ITS CONNECTION TO
THE CISTERCIAN ORDER
& KNIGHTS TEMPLAR

The Templars

There can be very little doubt that since their inception in, or around, 1118 the Knights Templar, as an Order, operated a two-tier system of membership. There existed an "Inner House" whose beliefs were very much at odds with Roman Catholicism generally practised by the members of the Order in those days, and there is strong evidence that the members chosen to be admitted to the teachings of this "inner house" were in fact being initiated into the secret mysteries of Saint Sophia (it is no coincidence that the Greek word for Wisdom is Sophia). A garbled version of these teachings eventually prompted, with an element of truth, the charges of heresy which were brought against the Knights Templar by Philip IV of France in 1307.

It was possible to maintain a secret "inner house" because the Templars were essentially a mystery school – that is, that they operated as a hierarchy that was based on initiation and secrecy. It is therefore likely that not only that a Templar of rank and file, who was no more than the simple Christian soldier he appeared to be, knew considerably less than his superiors, but that his actual beliefs were very different from those members of the "inner house".

The "inner house" appears to have existed in order to

further active research into esoteric and religious matters. Perhaps one of the reasons for their secrecy was the fact that they dealt with the arcane aspects of the Jewish and Islamic worlds. They sought, literally, the secrets of the universe wherever they suspected they might be found and in due course of their geographical and intellectual wanderings came to tolerate-perhaps even to embrace-some very unorthodox beliefs.

Amongst the unorthodox and "heretical" beliefs attributed to some of the "inner house" was the Johannite' heresy which held John the Baptist as the real Messiah, with Christ being seen as a usurper and a false prophet. It has been suggested that Hugh de Payen himself was a Johannite, and the |Order was known to have held John the Baptist in particular high regard.

Research has shown that the "inner house", within the leadership of the Templars, actually predates their "official " beginnings and it has been argued that the whole Templar movement was created in order to give the members of this "inner house" a public face.

As both the Templars and the Cistercian Order developed in parallel, one can discern a certain amount of deliberate co-ordination between them, and it has even been suggested that the Templars and the Cistercians were acting together according to a pre-arranged plan to take over Christendom.

The Cistercians

It is quite possible that the same two-tier system of membership had, for some time, existed in the monastic Cistercian Order, before the establishment of the Knights Templar, and that the secret teachings of Saint Sophia, or Holy Wisdom, were well known or practised by selected monks of high standing, which would account for St.

Bernard's knowledge and possible influence on the "inner workings" of the Temple Order.

St. Bernard was described as a fanatical worshiper of the cult of Saint Mary, and Christian Madonna and Child.

Sculptures adorned the majority of Cistercian Monasteries throughout Europe.

These sculptures, often depicted and known as the Black Madonna and Child, have variously been described as being of Saint Sophia (the Mother of Wisdom) or of Isis with her child Horus or, most importantly to the Knights Templar, as being of Mary Magdalene with the daughter of Jesus (on the basis that Jesus married Mary Magdalene and had issue).

Saint Mary Magdalene, (who together with Saint John the Baptist became the Patron Saints of the Hospitaller Order of Saint John of Jerusalem). Was venerated by the Templars, and was synonymous to them with Saint Sophia, who was found in all the great "Notre Dame" (Our Lady) cathedrals jointly built by the Templars and the Cistercians. The Catholic Church has always had difficulty in admitting that "Notre Dame" referred to Mary Magdalene and not Mary the mother of Jesus. It is worthy of note that when Grand Master Jacques de Molay was going to be burnt at the stake he asked to be turned towards the cathedral of Notre Dame.

St. Bernard of Clairvaux was thought to be well versed in the teachings of Holy Wisdom, and was personally responsible for the creation of the Rule for the Knights Templar, it may be therefore reasonably assumed that his knowledge of Saint Sophia influenced the doctrines of the Order and became inculcated into the rituals of the "inner house" of the Knights Templar and that these secret teachings spread, with the advance and growth of both the Cistercian Order and the Knights Templar, to most of Europe and the Near East, but always in a covert manner.

The Nizari Ismailis (Assassins)

In form, the Ismailis were a secret society with a system of oaths and initiations and a graded hierarchy of rank and knowledge. The Nine Degrees of Wisdom were the steps taken by the "Assasins" (Nizari Ismailis of the 11th century) in their endeavour to reach , through an exalted spiritual teaching, a full understanding of Wisdom.

The medieval Ismaili doctrine included an electic mix, it combined advanced philosophical speculation with Persian, Jewish, and Christian esotericism: Gnostic, neo-Platonic, Buddhist and Hindi mysticism: and elements of Sufi and Islamic cultism.

As a persecuted sect, the Ismailis were required to cloak their religious practises in the utmost secrecy. The chosen priesthood of teachers, the da'I, risked execution should a student panic and betray his teacher to the authorities.

The Assassin mystics mirrored the Templars in several striking ways. They both lived as warriors, following similarly austere and ascetic spiritual credos. They both emphasised religious purpose, courage, obedience and military duties, and both recruited from a middling, manorial class of men. The hierarchical structures of the two brotherhoods were also parallel:

Templar Grade	*Assassin equivalent*
Lay brother	lasiq (layman)
Sergeant	fida'I (agent)
Knight	rafiq (companion)
Prior	da'i
Grand Prior	da'i kabir
Grand Master	(Sheik) Grand Master

There was at this time, an intermittent, but close, connection between the Assassins and the Knights Templar, to whom the Assassins paid an annual tribute, and there is a persuasive " case for the influence of Ismaili teachings into Europe where those members of the Templar "inner house managed to escape the persecution of the Order. The Templars quietly continued to teach the secret doctrines and mystic techniques they had learned and developed in the Near East – the true secret teachings of Saint Sophia, and those gathered from the Ismaili Assassins.

It has further been stated that the Order of the Temple was indeed constituted of seven "exterior" degrees dedicated to the minor mysteries, and three "interior" degrees corresponding to the initiation into the great mysteries. This seems remarkably close to the Ismaili's mystery system and there is every reason to suppose that an exchange of philosophical ideas, between the Assassins and the Templars, took place at various times during the 12th and 13th century.

When the Order of the Temple was eventually persecuted by Philip IV there is very slender historical evidence to support the idea that the Knights Templar were ever effectively killed off. They would, in fact, have gone underground to regroup and reform. The very manner of their dissolution virtually guaranteed it.

Remember that the rank and file were very different from the members of the "inner house" the elite knights, who not only ran the organisation, but were also a repository for secret knowledge.

It is very likely that the members of both the "rank and file", and those of the "inner house" who practised the secret doctrines of saint Sophia, went off and founded their own underground movements, effectively starting two separate organisations, each claiming to have the true Templar pedigree.

The Knights of Saint Sophia

The Knights of Saint Sophia (or Knights of Holy Wisdom), as they were known from around the 9th century, have been linked to the Holy Roman Emperors since the days of Charlemagne, although there are those who are convinced that their philosophical ancestry goes back even further, via the Merovingian dynasties, to a Jewish sect , the Essenes. The Holy Roman Emperors were deemed to be the hereditary masters of the Order. The Knights of Saint Sophia were all deemed to be members of the "Confraternity of Mary Magdalene", and introduced the veneration of Saint Mary Magdalene to the Knights Templar. According to the Orders' traditions Mary Magdalene was regarded as the "Sophia" of Jesus.

It would seem therefore, that the teachings of Holy Wisdom, in the form of Saint Sophia must, at some time around the 11th century, have split with one branch, the Knights of Saint Sophia, staying within the province of the Holy Roman Emperors whilst the other branch, the teachings of Saint Sophia, flourished through the Cistercians and the Templars.

The split became obvious when, in September 1228, the Holy Roman Emperor, Frederick II, lead a crusade in the Holy Land. He was an extraordinary man who practised a very Gnostic type of "Christianity"; he was a great patron of the sciences, and of learning, with advanced views on economics, and was known by many as *Stupor Mundi* ('wonder of the world').

Frederick II was a religious sceptic who is said to have denounced Moses, Jesus and Mohammed as being "frauds and deceivers of mankind". He was, for his sins, excommunicated, not once but four times. Pope Gregory IX, called him the anti-Christ, thereby dividing the loyalties of the Christians in the Holy Land along Papal/Imperial lines. At this point the Templars aligned themselves with the Pope whilst the Teutonic Knights sided with the Emperor.

After his death his followers believed that there would be a "second coming" with him as Messiah, and that he would rule a 1000-year reich. Frederick II, Master of the Knights of Saint Sophia, died peacefully on the 13th December 1250 wearing the habit of a Cistercian monk thereby demonstrating, to those in the know, that they both (he and the Cistercian Order) shared the sacred teachings of Saint Sophia (Holy Wisdom).

The antipathy between the Holy Roman Emperors and the Popes was to continue, off and on, for the next 300 years, and it became particularly evident again during the reign of Rudolph II,

Martin Luther and Charles V, Holy Roman Emperor

In April 1521 Hermann von Hoff (1491-1554), the Captain of Muhlburg Castle (the oldest castle in Thurringia) Gleichen Burg Castle and Wachsenburg Castle, supplied an escort of 70 crossbow men, and accompanied Martin Luther (10.11.1482-18.02.1546) for his protection, to meet Charles V (Holy Roman Emperor) at the Reichstag at Worms, thereby establishing a link between the two families which was to be both on-going and strong. In 1541 Charles V granted Hermann, who was nominally a Roman Catholic, the title of Freiherr (Baron). His son Friedrich, Frieherr von Hoff (1517-1585) was however a strong supporter of the Lutheran cause and in 1538 joined the ranks of the Schmalkaldic League.

Emperor Rudolph II, Holy Roman Emperor.

It was Rudolph II of Habsburg 1552-1612 (Holy Roman Emperor) who, during his Mastership, re-named the Knights of Saint Sophia and, from which time, the Order became known as "The Most Illustrious and Sacred Congregation of the Military and Religious Knights of the Order of Saint Sophia". His choice of this name for the Order must be understood against a background of increasing militancy between the various opposing factions of the Christian church, and a time when both conservative old and radical new philosophies were being preached and discussed.

Although Rudolph II ostensibly tried to promote Roman Catholicism in Bohemia, he supported many Lutheran teachings, and was also renowned for his interest in alchemy, espousing many Gnostic ideas, as a consequence of which, in his later years, he experienced a very strained relationship with the Roman Catholic Church.

As he did not trust that the secrets of the order of Saint Sophia would be safe in the hands of his Imperial successor and brother, Matthias 1557-1619, the Emperor sought a kindred spirit, some who understood and shared his Gnostic philosophy and had an interest in matters alchemical, to succeed him as the hereditary Master. The Bohemian nobleman to whom the Emperor entrusted this responsibility, was Fra Henrik, Baron von Hoff, as he became known from that time onwards, (1555-1633). Fra Henrik, a highly placed member of the Emperor's court, was appointed master in 1590, to hold this Office, together with his descendants , until such time as it was deemed safe for the Order to be, once again, ruled by the Holy Roman Emperors.

He also appointed the Master to be the hereditary

"guardian" of the Philosopher's Stone" (*lapis elixir*). The "Philosophers Stone" is that tangible manifestation or actualisation of the inner potential of the spirit towards the highest, most abstract state. Thus the spirit tends towards the highest state of spiritual evolution, which is symbolically represented by gold. Just as the spirit is the most subtle and intangible aspect of man, so must we cause its faculties and potentials to manifest themselves downward into tangible, physical existence so that our minds, which is the emanation from spirit into material realm, and our bodies, may be rejuvenated and restored in their original purity. Hence the "Philosopher's Stone" was born, an alchemical concept, with its secrets, which were of the greatest importance to the Emperor, and which were easily combined with the secret teaching of Holy Wisdom.

In 1597 Rudolph II appointed,, as his Imperial Mathematician, Tycho Ottesen Brahe 14.12.1546 – 24.10.1601 a Danish nobleman whom King Frederick of Denmark had considered as his most eminent scientist and astronomer. There is little doubt that during the two years, prior to his death in 1601, Brahe befriended Fra

Henrik and extolled him to the virtues of life in a "Protestant" Denmark. When, in 1633, Fra Henrik died, he was succeeded by his son, Fra Wilhelm, Baron von Hoff (1597 – 1678), who fought on behalf of the Protestant cause during the "30 year war".

It was six years after the death of Rudolph II that the Thirty Year War (1618 – 1648) between the Catholics and the Protestants commenced. Fra Wilhelm was succeeded as Master, by his son, Fra Andreas, Baron von Hoff (1631 – 1670) who was born in Prague. His brother, Hans Wentzel, Baron von Hoff (1636 – 1713) was the first of the family to travelled to Denmark, where he arrived in 1659. There he married

(1688) Catharina von Horn, a descendant of Martin Luther, thus again strengthening the ties between the two families. It was Fra Johan Anton, Baron von Hoff (1784 – 1861) the Great-Great-Great-Grand-Son of Fra Andreas, who also eventually moved to Denmark and brought the Order of Saint Sophia with him.

In view of the religious and political instability of the Habsburg Crown it was decide that the hereditary Mastership, and governance of the Order of saint Sophia, would remain in the hands of the then Master's family, and his successors. The current Master Fra John Gunnar Knud Mattia, Dudley (Freiherr) von Sydow, Baron von Hoff born in Denmark (1937 -), The Master is the 9th cousin of princess Ingrid of Sweden 1910 – 2000 (Queen Consort of Denmark), mother of Queen Margrethe II of Denmark. In 1993 His Imperial & Royal Highness Archduke Joseph Arpad von Hapsburg awarded the Master with a Knighthood in the Hungarian Order of Vitez, and also bestowed upon him the cross of Merit for service to Hungary and the Hapsburg Crown.

The connection between the Holy Roman Empire and the Master's ancestors had previously been strengthened through the marriage in Stuttgart (1721) of Wilhelmine Luise, Baroness von Hoff (1704 – 1780) daughter of Friedrich Ludwig, Baron von Hoff (1663 – 1729) to Johann Rudolph Hedwiger, Reichsgrafen von Sponeck 1681 – 1740 (count of the Holy Roman Empire).

The Swedish Rite

Interestingly enough, there has, over the past three hundred years, been a gradual coming together of the two aspects of the Order of Saint Sophia due to the long standing Templar influence in Denmark and the emergence of the "Swedish Rite" in the 18th century, under the patronage of

King Charles XIII of Sweden, and practised throughout Scandinavia and parts of northern Germany.

King Charles' library holds documents purporting to establish the continuation of the Templar Order after the burning of its last Grand Master, Jacques de Molay.

The Scandinavian system insists that it is the real, but covert, continuation of the original, mediaeval Order of the Temple and demonstrates and purports to be a most important link with the first Knights Templar. The system has a clandestine organisation within the organisation. This hidden group is known only to those who are accorded the privilege of joining the inner circle.

Overtly, the System is composed of eleven degrees. The crucial point is reached at the tenth degree (Very Enlightened Brother) whereafter a secret selection is made. All brothers who are admitted to the tenth degree hope that they may pass an examination which is part of the admission ritual for the eleventh degree. But in reality, most will fail the significant, but covert test.

Only a very few are selected and these then go through another and different form of initiation. Only to these chosen few is given the knowledge of their special status. Thereafter they may continue their way through the system by way of entry into a hidden level of the eleventh degree (Most Enlightened brother, Knight Commander of the Red Cross).

The Royal Order of Charles XIII which, although not a Masonic Order, is open to only 33 members, all of whom must hold the 11th degree of the Swedish Rite. The Lord and Master of this Order is His Majesty Carl XVI Gustav of Sweden.

The especially chosen brothers are the ones who form the interior fraternity. They are the group referred to as

The League of Canonical Knights of the Holy Sepulchre in Jerusalem of Our Lord Jesus Christ's Holy and Poor Temple Order.

It is more than possible that sometime between 1766 – 1772 Freiherr (Baron) Johann August von Starck (1741 - !816), the son of a Protestant pastor of Schwerin (Mecklenburg), instigated the above named order. The historical basis of the new Order was the citation of a passage by Archbishop William of Tyre which suggests that there existed, alongside the Knights Templar, an organisation of Canons or |Clerks of the Temple and that this body had been in possession of secret knowledge transmitted by the Essenes.

Charles XIII's confidential documents describe these Canonical Knights as the "secret brotherhood within the brotherhood, forever united with the Templar Order. Those in possession of this knowledge are a closed and secret fraternity, unknown to other brothers"

When in session, the League of Canonical Knights is referred to as the Sanhedrin and the Master is accorded the title of Father of Wisdom (the title originally adopted by the Essene for their Master). He refers to the secret brothers as his Beloved Sons.

It is quite possible that von Starch became aware of some of the teachings of the Order of Saint Sophia and decided to introduce this concept into the Swedish Rite under the name of The League of Canonical Knights. The similarity in concept between the Knights of Saint Sophia and The League of Canonical Knights is too close to be considered a coincidence, however, there is no evidence that the Canonical Knights were, or are, in possession of the true secret doctrines of the Order of Saint Sophia.

According to the archives, held by the Swedish Royal Family, there is a suggestion that in the eyes of Swedish

Freemasonry there has been a continuous transmission of secrets (perhaps viewed as knowledge – *gnosis*, and held as belief), down the centuries and leading back to the Knights Templar – and possibly beyond.

The Templars, whether in their mysterious delving beneath the soil of Jerusalem, or in the building of mathematically controlled churches, were clearly pursuing a goal. They had knowledge – *gnosis*. The "inner house" seemed to go to great lengths to preserve their secret knowledge..

As the respected New Testament scholar Dr. Hugh Schonfield has demonstrated, the Templars used the Essenic code known as the Atbash cipher. This is truly remarkable because it had been used, at the time of the Essenes, by the authors of some of the Dead Sea Scrolls, at least one thousand years before the foundation of the Templar Order.

Schonfield reveals that when the code is applied to the name of the mysterious severed-head idol allegedly worshipped by the Templars – Bahomet – then it transforms into the Greek word Sophia.

The Wisdom worshipped by the Templars was both sacred and precious to them, as it was to their mentors, the Cistercians. The "head" is thought by many to be emblematic of the severed head of their patron saint, John the Baptist.

-------ooo-------

Saint Clement, one of the Fathers of the early Church left some interesting writings. In *Stromata*, his most important work, he discusses a "higher knowledge" contained in Christianity. The instructed Christian, he says, is "the true Gnostic...the perfect Christian", whose faith, he tells us, is related to Knowledge. A viewpoint that would be shared and endorsed by many Holy Roman Emperors and a great number of selected Knights Templar and Cistercian monks.

It was Pope Leo X (11.12.1475 – 11.12.1521) who reputedly said "All ages can testify enough how profitable that fable of Christ hath been to us and our company"

30.03.2012

OTHER AZILOTH TITLES BY RAYMOND HUDSON

So You Think You Know About Freemasonry?

Among Non-Masons, especially the sensationalist type, and even among many Freemasons, there are many misconceptions and misunderstandings of the original objectives, so much so that much of the meaning of Freemasonic ritual has become blurred and confused. The original creators of this system of character building, harmonising with humanity, and of creating a better understanding of the individual's relationship to God - whatever he deems his God to be - were very intelligent individuals. They possessed a deliberate intent regarding the most suitable method of encouraging others to achieve these ideals. By this system of progression, it was hoped that man's understanding of himself and his God would lead eventually to a peaceful harmony throughout life. So great was its aims and construction that it received many imitators, some not quite achieving the ideals envisaged by the original creators. This book is an attempt to 'get back to basics', and will hopefully bring some additional light upon what the author considers the greatest method of self-improvement ever devised by man.

So You Think You Know About Chapter?

This book is the natural progression from Ray Hudson's acclaimed first work "So You Think You Know About Freemasonry", and concerns the origins, symbols and rituals of 'The Order of the Holy Royal Arch', which follows the three Craft Degrees in the 'Progressive Science' of Freemasonry. Filled with fascinating, little known facts, there is much here that will surprise even veteran members of 'Chapter'. Hudson writes that he is "neither Judge nor historian, but simply an avid researcher who must understand what it is he is doing and what he is paying for ...". But as an active member of all the mainstream Masonic Orders, plus a several lesser known ones (and having received high honours in most) there are few alive that can match his breadth of knowledge and experience. A book for all Freemasons, and others, who wish to understand the sublime symbolism and hidden history behind this most important Masonic Order.

Freemasonry: A Progressive Science

When first initiated into Freemasonry, very few candidates are aware of the number of Degrees or Orders that exist, or their relevance to the Craft or historical incidents. In this important book, Raymond Hudson reveals the full titles and range of over thirty Masonic groups, giving details of their different history, aims and philosophies. Some are open to all Master Masons, while membership of other lesser known or esoteric fraternities, is strictly 'by invitation only'. The result is an engrossing mélange of Chivalric Orders, Druids, Rosicrucians, Saxon Kings, Mithraic Mysteries, Essenes, and the Illuminati, with Hermetic heptads and the grandiloquently-named "Order of the Knight Masons, Elect Priests of the Universe". A fascinating, entertaining and informative read for Mason and non-Mason alike.

AZILOTH ||| BOOKS

Aziloth Books publishes a wide range of titles ranging from hard-to-find esoteric books - *Parchment Books* - to classic works on fiction, politics and philosophy - *Cathedral Classics*. Our newest venture is *Aziloth Books Children's Classics*, with vibrant new covers and illustrations to complement some of the world's very best children's tales. All our imprints are offered to the reader at a competitive price and through as many mediums and outlets as possible.

We are committed to excellent book production and strive, whenever possible, to add value to our titles with original images, maps and author introductions. With the premium on space in most modern dwellings, we also endeavour - within the limits of good book design - to make our products as slender as possible, allowing more books to be fitted into a given bookshelf area.

We are a small, approachable company and would love to hear any of your comments and suggestions on our plans, products, or indeed on absolutely anything.

Aziloth Books, Rimey Law, Rookhope, Co. Durham, DL13 2BL, England.
t: 01388-517600 e: info@azilothbooks.com w: www.azilothbooks.com

PARCHMENT BOOKS enshrines the concept of the oneness of all true religious traditions - that "the light shines from many different lanterns". Our list below offers titles from both eastern and western spiritual traditions, including Christian, Judaic, Islamic, Daoist, Hindu and Buddhist mystical texts, as well as books on alchemy, hermeticism, paganism, etc.. By bringing together such spiritual texts, we hope to make esoteric and occult knowledge more readily available to those ready to receive it. We do not publish grimoires or titles pertaining to the left hand path. Titles include:

The Prophet; The Madman: Parables & Poems	Khalil Gibran
Abandonment to Divine Providence	Jean-Pierre de Caussade
Corpus Hermeticum	G. R. S. Mead (trans.)
The Confession of St Patrick	St. Patrick
The Outline of Sanity	G. K. Chesterton
An Outline of Occult Science	Rudolf Steiner
Esoteric Christianity; Thought-Forms*	Annie Besant
The Teachings of Zoroaster	Shapurji A. Kapadia
The Spiritual Exercises of St. Ignatius	St. Ignatius of Loyola
Daemonologie	King James of England
A Dweller on Two Planets	Phylos the Thibetan
Bushido*	Nitobe Inazo
The Interior Castle	St. Teresa of Avila
Songs of Innocence & Experience*	William Blake
The Secret of the Rosary	St. Louis Marie de Montfort
From Ritual to Romance	Jessie L. Weston
The God of the Witches	Margaret Murray
Kundalini – an occult experience	George S. Arundale
The Kingdom of God is Within You	Leo Tolstoy
The Trial and Death of Socrates	Plato
A Textbook of Theosophy	Charles W. Leadbetter
Chuang Tzu: Daoist Teachings	Chuang Tzu
Practical Mysticism	Evelyn Underhill
Tao Te Ching (Lao Tzu's 'Book of the Way')	Tzu, Lao
The Most Holy Trinosophia	Le Comte de St.-Germain
Tertium Organum	P. D. Ouspensky
Totem and Taboo	Sigmund Freud
The Kebra Negast	E. A. Wallis Budge
Esoteric Buddhism	Alfred Percy Sinnett
Demian: the story of a youth	Hermann Hesse

* with colour illustrations

Obtainable at all good online and local bookstores.
View Aziloth Books' full list at: www.azilothbooks.com

CATHEDRAL CLASSICS hosts an array of classic literature, from erudite ancient tomes to avant-garde, twentieth-century masterpieces, all of which deserve a place in your home. All the world's great novelists are here, Jane Austen, Dickens, Conrad, Arthur Machen and Henry James, brushing shoulders with such disparate luminaries as Sun Tzu, Marcus Aurelius, Kipling, Friedrich Nietzsche, Machiavelli, and Omar Khayam. A small selection is detailed below:

Frankenstein	Mary Shelley
Herland; With Her in Ourland	Charlotte Perkins Gilman
The Time Machine; The Invisible Man	H. G. Wells
Three Men in a Boat	Jerome K Jerome
The Rubaiyat of Omar Khayyam	Omar Khayyam
A Study in Scarlet; The Sign of the Four	Arthur Conan Doyle
The Picture of Dorian Gray	Oscar Wilde
Flatland	Edwin A. Abbott
The Coming Race	Bulwer Lytton
The Adventures of Sherlock Holmes	Arthur Conan Doyle
The Great God Pan	Arthur Machen
Beyond Good and Evil	Friedrich Nietzsche
England, My England	D. H. Lawrence
The Castle of Otranto	Horace Walpole
Self-Reliance, & Other Essays (series1&2)	Ralph W. Emmerson
The Art of War	Sun Tzu
A Shepherd's Life	W. H. Hudson
The Double	Fyodor Dostoyevsky
To the Lighthouse; Mrs Dalloway	Virginia Woolf
The Sorrows of Young Werther	Johann W. Goethe
Leaves of Grass - 1855 edition	Walt Whitman
Analects	Confucius
Beowulf	Anonymous
The Subjection of Women	John Stuart Mill
The Rights of Man	Thomas Paine
Progress and Poverty	Henry George
Captain Blood	Rafael Sabatini
Captains Courageous	Rudyard Kipling
The Meditations of Marcus Aurelius	Marcus Aureliu
The Social Contract	Jean Jacques Rousseau
War is a Racket	Smedley D. Butler
The Dead	James Joyce
The Old Wives' Tale	Arnold Bennett

Obtainable at all good online and local bookstores.
View Aziloth Books' full list at: www.azilothbooks.com

The Railway Children	Edith Nesbit
Anne of Green Gables	Lucy Maud Montgomery
What Katy Did	Susan Coolidge
Puck of Pook's Hill	Rudyard Kipling
The Jungle Books	Rudyard Kipling
Just So Stories	Rudyard Kipling
Alice Through the Looking Glass	Charles Dodgson
*Alice's Adventures in Wonderland**	Charles Dodgson
Black Beauty	Anna Sewell
The War of the Worlds	H. G Wells
The Time Machine	H. G .Wells
The Sleeper Awakes	H. G. Wells
The Invisible Man	H. G. Wells
The Lost World	Sir Arthur Conan Doyle
*Gulliver's Travels**	Jonathan Swift
Catriona (David Balfour)	Robert Louis Stevenson
The Water Babies	Charles Kingsley
The First Men in the Moon	Jules Verne
The Secret Garden	Frances Hodgson Burnett
A Little Princess	Frances Hodgson Burnett
*Peter Pan**	J. M. Barrie
*The Song of Hiawatha**	Henry W. Longfellow
Tales from Shakespeare	Charles and Mary Lamb
The Wonderful Wizard of Oz	L. Frank Baum
The Complete Grimm's Fairy Tales	Jacob & Wilhelm Grimm

Lightning Source UK Ltd.
Milton Keynes UK
UKHW021433040621
384935UK00004B/176